SECRETS
OF THE
APPLE TREE

Carron Brown

Illustrated by Alyssa Nassner

Kane Miller
A DIVISION OF EDC PUBLISHING

A tree is bustling with life.

If you look closely at its trunk,
branches, leaves, and fruit,
you will find the animals,
plants, and fungi living there.

Shine a flashlight behind the page,
or hold it to the light to reveal
what is hidden in and around the
tree. Discover a small world
of great surprises.

An apple tree is green
with leaves in summer.
Can you see what it looks like in winter?

Brrrrr ...

In winter, the branches are bare.

One by one, the leaves drift to
the ground in fall, but the tree will
grow new leaves in spring.

Many animals live
around the tree.

Can you see who
the bird is about
to grab?

Slithering, wriggling worms push
through the soil around the roots.

A tree's roots grow long and deep.
The roots soak up water from rain,
which helps to keep the tree alive.

The wind blows leaves off the tree.
Can you see who is resting
under this leaf pile?

Surprise! A toad stays cool and unseen in the dark under the leaves.

He lives in damp places, where there are many slugs, worms, and insects to eat.

Branches also fall from the tree to the ground below.

Can you find anything growing on this dead branch?

In dark, damp patches on the fallen branch, groups of mushrooms, toadstools, and other fungi grow.

The dead wood rots and makes food that they can eat.

Something runs quickly past the dead branch. It scurries behind a stone.

Who does this tail belong to?

Look!

A small, scaly lizard rests
between the stones.

It waits to catch a passing insect,
spider, slug, or snail for its dinner.

On the other side of the tree, a rabbit hops into a hole in the ground.

Where is he disappearing to?

Thump!
Thump! Deep down in the ground, rabbits dig nests and tunnels.

They build large burrows, where many rabbits can live together.

A fly whirs up
the tree trunk.

Something is
hiding on the
bark. Can you
see what it is?

A moth has settled on the tree. Its wings are the same color as the bark. As long as the moth stays very still, nothing will see it.

The fly isn't whirring around now.
It seems to be stuck in midair.

What's stopping it from
flying away?

It's a trap!

The fly has flown into
a spider web.

Its feet are really stuck
in strands of sticky silk.

The web is a trap that catches
food for the spider.

A bird flies through the rustling leaves with a worm in her beak. Who is going to eat the worm?

These hungry chicks will
soon gobble up the worm.

Tweet!
Tweet!

They hatched from eggs
in a nest that their parents
built in the tree.

Let's look a little
closer at the tree.

What's this hanging
from a branch?

# Buzz

Buzz

Buzz

Hundreds of bumblebees are busy making wax to build their nest.

Buzz

They also collect sweet nectar from flowers. They store it in their nest to make honey that they can eat.

Buzz

A loud noise has startled the moths from their hiding places.

Who is making such a racket?

Rat-a tat-a-tat!

Tap, tap, tapping away at the bark, a woodpecker drills again and again.

She makes a small hole in the bark with her beak. Quick as a flash, her tongue darts into the gap to grab a tasty insect.

This hole hasn't been made by a woodpecker—it's much too big.

Can you see who lives in this den?

Sshhh...

A squirrel is sleeping on a
bed of dried grass and leaves.
His long tail is curled tightly
by him to keep him warm.

The leaf is shaking. There's something on the other side enjoying a meal.

Can you see who's eating the leaf?

Munch!
Munch!

A furry caterpiller is eating and eating and eating. It eats so much because it needs food to help it become a beautiful butterfly.

Large, juicy red apples grow on the tree. These are the tree's fruits.

What's inside the apple?

Crunch!

The apple is very tasty, but the small, hard pieces inside don't taste as nice. These are the apple tree's seeds, and they aren't supposed to be eaten.

Ripe apples have
fallen from the tree.

Can you see
what happens
to apple seeds
that drop on
the ground?

Below the soil, an apple seed has split and grown roots.

The roots reach down to gather food and water. A shoot pushes up from the seed, and up through the soil.

Above the soil, a green
shoot grows up and up
toward the sun. In time,
it will become a tall,
strong tree, with a small
world all of its own.

There's more...

When you find a tree, look all around it and see who you can find.
Remember to look up as well as down.

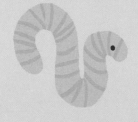

In the Soil Under the grassy surface, earthworms push and pull muscles along their bodies to move through the soil. The tunnels the worms make help water to reach plant roots.

Damp and dark Be careful when kicking leaves because toads might be resting there during the day. At night, toads hop around the trees, using their long, sticky tongues to catch their food.

In the cracks Lizards leave their hiding places under stones or logs to bask (sunbathe). They are cold-blooded animals, so they cannot make their own heat. They need the sun to warm them.

Burrowers Rabbits live together in burrows under the ground. They come to the surface in the early morning and evening to look for green plants (such as grass and clover) and tree bark to eat.

Hidden colors Moths and butterflies hide on trees, stones, and plants when they're not flying. Their folded wings cover their bright colors, and this helps to hide them from animals that want to eat them.

Web spinners Spiders spin webs using sticky silk made inside their body. Spiders sit by the side of the web until an insect gets stuck in it. Then they rush out, wrap the animal in silk, and eat it.

Up high Nests in tree hollows or on branches can be made using twigs, grass, mud, and moss. All birds hatch from eggs. Birds that live in trees eat slugs, snails, caterpillars and other insects, and fruits.

Buzzing Bumblebees build a nest for their queen, so she has a home for all her young. The bees work together to keep the nest clean, protect it, and to make enough honey to feed all the bees.

Cozy den Tree hollows, forks of branches, or old birds' nests can be squirrel dens. Squirrels line their dens with moss, dried grass, and feathers, and they sleep curled up together in winter for warmth.